Platform Papers

Quarterly essays from Currency House

No. 11: January 2007

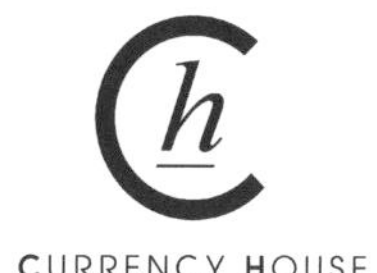

PLATFORM PAPERS
Quarterly essays from Currency House Inc.
Editor: Dr John Golder, j.golder@unsw.edu.au
Currency House Inc. is a non-profit association and resource centre advocating the role of the performing arts in public life by research, debate and publication.
Postal address: PO Box 2270, Strawberry Hills, NSW 2012, Australia
Email: info@currencyhouse.org.au Tel: (02) 9319 4953
Website: www.currencyhouse.org.au Fax: (02) 9319 3649

ISBN 978 0 97573 019 5
ISSN 1449-583X

Cover design by Kate Florance, Currency Press
Typeset in 10.5 Arrus BT
Printed by Hyde Park Press, Adelaide

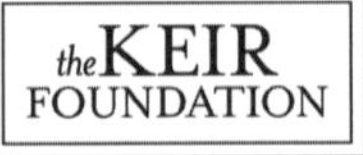

This edition of Platform Papers is supported by donations from the following: the Keir Foundation, Katharine Brisbane, Malcolm Duncan, David Marr, Tony Scotford, Alan Seymour, Mary Vallentine and Jane Westbrook. To them and to all our supporters Currency House extends sincere gratitude.

Contents

AVAILABILITY Platform Papers, quarterly essays on the performing arts, is published every January, April, July and October and is available through bookshops or by subscription. For order form, see page 54.

LETTERS Currency House invites readers to submit letters of 400–1,000 words in response to the essays. Letters should be emailed to the Editor at j.golder@unsw.edu.au or info@currencyhouse.org.au, or posted to Currency House at PO Box 2270, Strawberry Hills, NSW 2012, Australia. To be considered for the next issue, the letters must be received by 16 February 2007.

CURRENCY HOUSE For membership details, see our website at: www.currencyhouse.org.au

A Regional State of Mind

Making Art Outside Metropolitan Australia

LYNDON TERRACINI

The author

LYNDON TERRACINI made his debut as an operatic baritone with New Opera in South Australia in 1974 and joined the Australian Opera in 1975. His performance of Hans Werner Henze's solo work *El Cimarron* for the 1976 Adelaide Festival led to a successful career in the opera houses of Europe, Australia and New Zealand over thirty years. His roles have included Don Giovanni, Escamillo in *Carmen*, Marcello in *La Bohème* and Figaro in *The Marriage of Figaro*; but his special interest has been in the development of new work, with composers such as Louis Andriessen, Elliot Carter, Charles Ives, Dominic Muldowney, Hans Zender, Giorgio Battistelli, Peter Maxwell-Davies, Elena Kats-Chernin, Barry Conyngham, Brian Howard and Stephen Sondheim (for whom he played the title role in the Australian premiere of *Sweeney Todd*).

In 1988 he settled with his family in Lismore, where he established Northern Rivers Performing Arts (NORPA) and in 2000 was appointed Artistic Director/CEO of the biennial Queensland Music Festival. He travelled all over the state to commission and create music and theatre works for the festivals in 2001, 2003 and 2005, and was then appointed Artistic Director/CEO of the 2006 Brisbane Festival.

His influence has been extensive in the encouragement of Australian composers.

He holds two honorary doctorates from the Central Queensland and Southern Cross Universities; in 2001 received a music fellowship from the Australia Council, and in 2005 was awarded the Dame Elisabeth Murdoch Cultural Leadership Award by the Australian Business Arts Foundation.

Author's acknowledgements

I owe a special debt of gratitude to the thousands of artists, theatre workers, community and audience members who have been part of the projects with which I have been associated over the past thirty-three years, and who by doing so have given me so much joy.

I would also like to thank John Golder and Katharine Brisbane for the tremendous support and editorial assistance they have given me in the writing of this essay.

1
Introduction

This essay explores the role of culture, art and community in our lives. It also examines the making of Australian theatre. What is it? What does it mean? How does it relate to artists, audiences and the public in general? What effect does our community of artists have on who we are as Australians and the culture of our place? It also examines the structural composition of artistic management, as we endeavour to make Australian art in a disparate and complex landscape, striving to make sense of the changes currently taking place in regional and global communities.

What is the culture of our place, of our backyard? How is Brisbane different from Melbourne and why is Melbourne different from Sydney? We are a diverse nation living in very diverse places and we make art, often in spite of where we live, that expresses the culture of our place. Reflecting ourselves, seeing how we are defined by where we come from, is one of the great joys of making art.

If it's not too much of a contradiction in terms, I believe that making an Australian theatre—theatre in the broadest sense, that is—has been almost by design a process of accidental anarchy. Historically, from the beginnings of the colony, it has been a larrikin anti-establishment form of expression generated by its place and local culture. From that time to the present—via Ray Lawler's *Summer of the Seventeenth Doll*, Tim Winton's *Cloudstreet* and, much more recently, the Brisbane Festival production of David Malouf's *Johnno*—we have responded to work which is about us, about who we are and where we live.

My work with Northern Rivers Performing Arts (NORPA), then with the Queensland Music Festival (QMF) and last year with Brisbane Festival has led me, over the past fifteen years, on a journey of discovery, learning more and more about the strong links that bind people to 'their places'. Every town and city, even every suburb, I have found, has not only its own history, but also its own individual culture. The opportunity to create work which reflects a local culture, the culture of particular places, has been a privilege and a most fascinating experience.

That journey began in December 1993, when at NORPA I adapted Peter Weir's film of *The Cars that Ate Paris* as a large-scale, outdoor musical; and it succeeded because it reflected the feral culture which was so powerful around Lismore and Byron Bay at the time. It was staged against the wall of Lismore city hall and the street outside, where I directed stock cars and Mad-Max buggies to drive around the closed-off street. Other musicals followed. A decade later *Bob Cat Magic* and *Bob Cat Dancing* in Mt Isa celebrated the heavy machinery culture of that place, as did the heritage elements of *Charters Towers—The Musical*. These three pieces have been very successful with their audiences for the Queensland Music Festival.

The depth of local knowledge held by so many people has astonished me when putting together the program for Brisbane Festival 2006. Each suburb has its historical society and its stories of place. The outcome of this research contributed a surprisingly large body of work from a variety of communities. We made theatre pieces about the cultures of all those individual suburbs, about those places and the people who choose to live there.

The Brisbane suburb of Coorparoo has a skate park; used by skaters from all over Brisbane, it is well known throughout Australia as a meeting place for competitive skateboarders. After getting a feel for the suburb, talking with the local councillor and observing the activity in this terrific skate park, I decided to call our show *Coorparoo Sk8*. As a basis we used a script by playwright Janis Balodis, which had been performed by NORPA in 1999. *Coorparoo Sk8* employed the language and the form of hip hop, the physicality of break-dance, and the sounds of street culture.

Coorparoo Sk8 is the story of three aliens who land in Coorparoo in search of the quintessential Aussie. It is all about outsiders, people who don't quite fit the common notion or the system. Composer Shenton Gregory's score reflected the skate culture of the local suburban streets and included just about everything—rockabilly, reggae, stadium rock, punk, ska—except classical music. With a live band playing on an enormous two-level stage shaped like a ghetto blaster, the show included BMX bikers, in-line skaters and mountain bikers. It proved a powerful connector between an international arts festival and the street culture of a small corner of Brisbane

The suburb of Zillmere provided another challenge. This area of Brisbane has a large population of Pacific Islanders and with them we developed *Paradise—The Musical*, the result of a ten-week workshop involving Backbone Youth Arts, Breakthrough (a youth development organisation that works mainly with Pacific Islander communities) and Visible Ink. The sports ground of the Zillmere State School was transformed into a mythical island in the South Pacific, where two tribes are at war over the island's inadequate and fast-dwindling resources, severely reduced by the effects of global warming. Enter Richard Sunderland, an international entrepreneur, anxious to make money by building a holiday resort in this undiscovered paradise. *Paradise—The Musical* was an ambitious project: not only did it resonate in a profound way with the local community and provide a real sense of connection between the culture of the South Pacific and of suburban Zillmere, but also, by introducing issues of global warming, it sought to link local issues to national—indeed, international—issues. As such, *Paradise—The Musical* sat at the very heart of the 2006 Brisbane Festival as I conceived it. But more of this presently.

2
How do we define a local culture?

For an outsider like myself, entering a new community and trying to identify exactly what constitutes its particular culture can be intimidating. It is rarely what one expects and usually a lot more subtle and surprising. While I was Artistic Director of the Queensland Music Festival, I would visit every town where we intended to stage a large event in order to get a feel of the place. I would go to the pub and have a beer with the locals, talk to cab drivers (if the town was large enough to have a taxi) and chat informally to as many people as I could. I would then talk to the mayor and lots of other residents, in an effort to gauge as distinctly as I could just what it was that made the heart of each of these towns beat. Earlier this year, when I was preparing the across-Brisbane program, I did the same thing in the various suburbs of Brisbane.

In 2003, we commissioned composer Sarah Hopkins to write a piece for the town of Childers in south-west Queensland. Childers is a small National Trust town with a population of some 2,500, in the sugar-cane country just west of Bundaberg, and is internationally remembered for the tragic fire in 2000 at the Palace Backpackers Hostel, in which fifteen young tourists died. As it slowly recovered from this tragedy, Childers was totally unprepared for the emotional and cultural connection that the making of art can demonstrate. We did not set out to create a piece which would enable a community to openly grieve. However, it was apparent that the process of rehearsing and presenting this piece gave the community a sense of release.

At the first performance, on 27 July 2003, the members of the community choir had tears streaming down their cheeks as they sang Sarah's piece, *Childers Shining*. It had an extraordinary impact. The piece comprised thirty minutes of visionary music, nine songs for choir, orchestra, didgeridoo and celestial harmonic whirlies. Conducted by Robert Rotar, the massed choirs and orchestra, which seemed to involve the entire community, consisted of the Childers Choral Society, the Woodgate Singers, the Orpheus Singers, the Bundaberg Youth Choir, the Bundaberg Youth Orchestra and Childers State students. The text itself was unconnected to the tragedy; in fact, much of what the choir sang were sounds which Sarah herself had devised, but the whole had an inspiring and uplifting effect on both the singers and the packed auditorium. As a result, in 2005 Sarah wrote a sequel for the QMF; it was called *Childers Shining—One World*. The response to this was, if anything, even more powerful.

The impact of these two performances was brought home to me a few weeks later. At the end of September 2005 I received a fax from the Isis Shire Council. They had received an application from a developer who was keen to build a new sub-division in Childers and wanted to call it 'Childers Shining'. The main street was to be called 'One World' and a street running from it 'Sarah Hopkins Lane'. Creating a new work for that place, about Childers and its people, has had lasting influence upon the whole district. Indeed, there's a mosaic in the footpath of the new development incorporating parts of Sarah's score.

A permanent memorial of a very different kind is the Winton Musical Fence. Winton is an isolated small town in sheep and cattle country in central Queensland, chiefly known for its association with two Australian icons. It's where Banjo Paterson's 'Waltzing Matilda' was performed for the first time, and it was at the Winton Club, in 1921, that the first board meeting was held of the Queensland and Northern Territory Aerial Service, today known as Qantas. The Musical Fence is located on the edge of the town, on the site of the first Qantas landing on a flight from Longreach, and was the initiative of QMF in association with the Winton Shire Council. Built during the 2003 and 2005 festivals by the Melbourne musician, Graeme Leak, who both designed and oversaw its construction, the fence has been described as a 'vertically hung 50-metre xylophone'.

It is made, not surprisingly, from everyday fencing wire. Its fence-posts, similar to those on virtually every outback fence, are made from the gidji tree, which grows prolifically throughout western Queensland. The wood from the gidji tree is extremely strong and resistant to all pests as well as the harsh climate of the area. The fence has four strands of wire, which are 'strained' horizontally, and a tool known as a fence strainer is used to tune it. The wires are tightened or loosened to adjust the pitch in the same way as a piano-tuner tunes a piano. Each wire is tuned to a different pitch to facilitate the playing of melody and chords. No special skill or knowledge is required to play it; it is an instrument that can be played by anyone in any number of ways—bowed, struck, vibrated, or punished in any way one chooses. The sound is amplified by sounding boards which are attached to the fence from above and look rather like those 'spoilers' that are fixed to the roofs of speedway racing cars. When it is idle it is played by the wind blowing across the plains of western Queensland. To hear this sound is a wonderfully eerie experience.

When Graeme finally completed the first section of the fence, just before the QMF in 2003, he was having a beer with the builder. 'Well, that's all good, mate', said the builder, 'but can you play a tune on it?' 'Sure', replied Graeme, 'What would you like to hear? Since we're in Winton, what about "Waltzing Matilda"?' So, at sunset in the middle of that great open plain, underneath the big sky that is western Queensland, Graeme played 'Waltzing Matilda' for him on the Winton Musical Fence.

It must have been a magical performance, and sadly I wasn't there to hear it. But the story goes that when Graeme had finished, the builder leant back and exclaimed, 'Bugger me!' Then, without another word, he jumped into his ute and drove off, swirls of dust billowing from the wheels. Graeme was mortified. Believing all his hard work had gone for nothing, he began to pack up his gear. Five minutes later, however, more clouds of dust announced the ute's return—but now it had half-a-dozen blokes hanging out the back. It skidded to a halt, and the motley group jumped down and asked Graeme if he could play 'Melancholy Baby'. He was kept there playing requests until midnight.

Since the world premiere performance of the Musical Fence in 2003 an average of over twenty carloads of tourists per day have visited it. Children beg their grandparents to take them to it, and they play it for hours on end. It is open every day and is free.

That year we formed the Winton Musical Fence Band for QMF and the enthusiastic members of the local community were instructed by Graeme in the art of fence-playing. Three years later this wonderful group are still playing together and are now proficient fence-players.

The idea for a Musical Fence in Winton came to me while driving through that extraordinary landscape, day after day, seemingly never to reach that distant horizon. In that big-sky country, I realised, people are connected not by the roads that bisect the landscape, but by the fences which delineate the massive properties they inhabit. People meet at their common boundary, the fence. It's there that they discuss prime cattle, tractors, grain—and everything else. The fence is their meeting place. I believe that this is the reason why the Winton Musical Fence has been so successful: its sound is the soul of that country community.

■

Barcaldine may be a sleepy town of just over 1,700 people, some 1,080 kilometres north-west of Brisbane, but it is justly celebrated as the site of the 1891 shearers' strike, which is credited as being one of the factors leading to the formation of the Australian Labor Party. It was there, one morning at dawn, underneath the Tree of Knowledge, that we created the Barcaldine Big Marimba Band to open the QMFs of 2001 and 2003. Trees are valued in Barcaldine because there are so few of them. Every street is named after a tree, and the Tree of Knowledge has arguably been Australia's most important tree. ALP mythology has it that the first Labor branch was founded at a meeting of striking pastoral workers under the ghost gum. It seemed that a musical instrument connected to this iconic tree would, literally, resonate with the local community. In the months leading up to the festival, Mick Moore and Jacinta Foale conducted workshops for the two hundred locals who made up the Barcaldine Marimba Band in how to play this remarkable cousin to the xylophone. The band members also took part in instrument-making workshops, and went on to build for themselves seventy marimbas from Queensland hoop pine. As the sun rose over the town, the entire shire population turned out to hear the Mornington Island Songmen chant in the day and open the festival. Later, the Big Marimba Band performed with Dutch percussion ensemble, Anumadutchi.

The event was hugely successful, and had both major and minor repercussions. Two years later other outback councils queued up to become part of the 2003 QMF. The festival had given an enormous boost to community spirit and put Barcaldine on the tourist map, with consequent economic benefits. But it also gave extended life to the Big Band, which still continues to thrive. It played at the opening event at the QMF in 2005 in Winton, and gives regular performances throughout the vast areas of western Queensland, making music that reflects the culture of their big backyard.

For me a festival is like a great tree. It's a meeting place, and throughout our history important meetings have taken place under great trees. A great tree also provides a canopy where young seedlings are protected from the sun and can, in time, grow to replace the older tree. They then provide shelter for the next generation, and so the cycle continues. That is also the role of a great festival, to nourish and provide shelter for smaller arts organisations and individual artists, so that they too can grow and flourish.

3
Festivals and place

A festival that is focused on the culture of place, however, needs to be about a lot more than setting a play in a particular area, city or region. It should be about fundamentally understanding what resonates within the people who live there, left there, or died there; and about translating those deep local associations for the benefit of a much wider audience. It should also be a place where big ideas take root, where inspirational individuals and artists who believe passionately in their cultural and artistic responsibilities can plant seeds that will grow to nourish the minds of a broader community.

David Malouf's iconic novel, *Johnno*, is a profound reflection on the culture of post-war Brisbane, and its impact today is as potent as when it was first published just over thirty years ago. It's about all those people who left the city, vowing never to return, and the large numbers of them who, having left, have been unable, as Johnno so delicately puts it, 'to shit Brisbane out of their system'. And it is *because* the vividness of its sense of locality is then endorsed by the reader's relationship with their own experience of place that a work like *Johnno* can move beyond the constituency that inspired it to embrace the universal.

The Eighth Wonder is an opera by Alan John and Dennis Watkins about the architect of the Sydney Opera House, Jørn Utzon, and the controversy surrounding his dismissal in 1966—a drama that still resonates among Sydneysiders. The first performance of the opera was a unique experience in that it was held inside the building which was its subject. A work more physically tied to place would be extremely difficult to find. And, in the world of contemporary opera and music theatre, for which audience numbers are traditionally small, *The Eighth Wonder* did extremely well. It was a singularly moving experience to walk away from the Sydney Opera House at the conclusion of that opening performance back in 1995 and then to look back at that phenomenal building while the music was still cascading through the memory. The qualities one retains of *The Eighth Wonder* do not confine it to the place in which it was created. It will be interesting to see how strongly the work is able to resonate in other places, in other countries.

The Festivals Australia Regional Residencies is a Government cultural program that provides assistance to regional and remote communities to 'tell their stories and the stories of their communities' at local festivals and major one-off community celebrations. It is fine and notable initiatives such as this, and the Australia Council's New Australian Stories, which provides funding for work specifically about Australians, that make it possible for us to bring our work, not only to other local communities, but to a broader, international community. It's the telling of our stories about ourselves and about our places that define our theatre and our culture. And it is this, I believe, that will ultimately lead the international community to understand and respect that culture. Malouf's *Johnno* speaks directly to us Australians, but it also has a strong international resonance. This is why I commissioned Stephen Edwards to adapt the novel, with a score by Elena Kats-Chernin, to mark the opening of the Brisbane Festival last July. And why it is wonderfully appropriate that *Johnno*, a co-production by the festival, Brisbane's La Boite Theatre Company and England's Derby Playhouse—and with financial assistance from the New Australian Stories program—will bring to British audiences at the Derby Playhouse this February and March the adventures of Johnno and Dante in Brisbane in the forties and fifties.

Winners, which opened at the festival just eight days after *Johnno*, was a project of a quite different order. Co-produced with Fabrica, the Italian arts and communications resource centre, composed and conducted by Andrea Molino, Fabrica Musica's Artistic Director, and directed by myself, it was a monumental production that integrated audio/video links with musicians, singers, performers and excerpts of video interviews with people around the world connected to an historical or recent event related to the theme of 'winners and losers', e.g. Sharpeville in 1960, New York in 2001 and Maralinga, South Australia, in the 1950s. In a word, *Winners* tackled one of those big ideas that are the business of festivals, issues that connect us at both the local and the global levels. In October last year it travelled to the Pompidou Centre in Paris, where it had its European premiere.

■

During September and early October last year, I was invited to be part of a five-member international jury for the Venice Biennale for Music. What to me was remarkable about the ten days I spent in Venice was how clearly this peculiar phenomenon of the 'culture of place' was demonstrated in the works presented—even in La Fenice, its celebrated opera house. Perhaps it was *The City of Falling Angels*, John Berendt's extraordinary account of the rebuilding of La Fenice after its destruction by arson in 1996 that put the thought in my head, but it was a devotion to the culture of place that dictated to the Venetians that, however long it took, the theatre had to be restored to its former glory. Its baroque splendour is very much a reflection of the city: like Sydney minus its Opera House, Venice minus La Fenice was unthinkable.

I was not the only one aware of this, or of the way in which the theatre's directors were planning next season's program. There was considerable discussion about work that genuinely reflected the composer's origins and the differences between composers such as Swiss-born Beat Furrer, to whom we ultimately awarded the Golden Lion Prize, and someone like the classical German composer, Wolfgang Rihm, could not have been more noticeable. It was interesting to recognise how Robert Ashley's music resonated in such a 'Californian' manner and how Jonathan Dove and Thomas Ades were so English in their articulation and communication. These associations between the work and its place of origin did not affect the final judging, but they did provide the catalyst for some particularly interesting and revealing artistic discussions.

One of the other judges for the Leone d'Oro was Gianpaolo Vianello, Director of La Fenice. We had long conversations about the culture of place and about how, over the next two seasons, the celebrated opera house intended to give special emphasis to that subject. A new opera has been commissioned about the life of Carlo Goldoni, the prolific eighteenth-century playwright who was born in Venice and whose comedies make rich use of Venetian dialect and colloquialism. This piece will have its world premiere later this year at La Fenice, which is just around the corner from the theatre that bears Goldoni's name. Later in the season La Fenice will present a new production of Verdi's *Simone Boccanegra*, which, of course, is also set in Venice. Indeed, the action takes place primarily in the Doge's Palace, also little more than a stone's throw from the opera house. These are productions that will forge intimate links with the culture of Venice and it is hoped that they will go on to have a wider and universal artistic resonance.

It was the same story in Russia, which I visited on my way to Italy. Moscow's Bolshoi Theatre was planning new productions of Mussorgsky's *Boris Godunov* and Tchaikovsky's *Eugene Onegin*, two great pillars of Russia's musical culture. Much of the action of *Boris Godunov* is set in Moscow, either in the Novodievichy Monastery, or else either in the square in the Kremlin or various Kremlin interiors. Walking past Pushkin Square, where the famous writer's statue stands majestically surveying that great city, I couldn't help but sing in my head the music Tchaikovsky wrote for Pushkin's text. If this is the effect the statue had on me, one can only envy the Russian audiences the effect that those extraordinary works must have on them. And the same again in St Petersburg, where I was fortunate to be able to attend a performance of Tchaikovsky's *Pique Dame*, also after a story by Pushkin, at the little-known Mikhailovsky Theatre. This intensely Russian piece often sounds strange to Western audiences, but played to its own audience, who were hearing it sung in their native language, gave it the authority of belonging. The strings particularly in Russian orchestras sound very different from those in a European orchestra and that difference really had a demonstrable effect on this production. The tenor was outstanding and the communication between the stage and the audience was palpable. It was exciting and strangely moving to be sitting amongst people so completely involved in the performance.

To create work that has important cultural significance to a particular place and people, and which is then embraced universally as an important artistic creation, is what every artist strives for. It's the pursuit of that elusive state that we define as art; it's our eternal quest.

■

Place, of course, can be as small as a country town, a street or even a building, but place at a festival can also be as big as the world. Brisbane Festival 2006 was designed to reflect the cultural and artistic landscape of the city of Brisbane and the state of Queensland. It was a 'meeting place' at which to celebrate and encourage dialogue articulated musically, theatrically and through many other forms of cultural and artistic expression; but it was essentially a coming together of people from every part of Brisbane, Queensland and Australia, as well as a significant number of international visitors. Consequently, the inclusion in the festival program of *Earth Dialogues Brisbane* was a natural extension of the cultural world which Brisbane Festival 2006 embraced. It seemed an exciting—and very timely—idea to have as a centrepiece to the festival a World Forum for Resource Management, Climate Change and Sustainable Development.

At the beginning of the twenty-first century, resource management, sustainable development, climate change, and energy security are the major issues affecting our planet. These are the issues which can and will change people's lives, and to change people's lives is what we, as artists, strive for in every work that we make.

There are countless examples of artists creating work which resonates far beyond the art gallery or opera house. However, at this moment in history, as our country—indeed, our planet—faces an alarming future, artists have no greater responsibility than that of joining hands with the sciences in order to face the challenge. Reconnecting the humanities and the sciences was an integral part of the philosophy of Brisbane Festival 2006. We needed to address these issues passionately and we were committed to reactivating that connection and, indeed, to stimulating the process of thought-creation which encourages imaginative and creative artistic and scientific thinking.

As I have already said, the effect of global warming and unsympathetic development upon the Pacific was a central issue in *Paradise—The Musical* and one example of how those connections between the arts and the sciences can be established. But the festival presented us with an opportunity to place a major focus on the planet's most urgent need, namely 'for the ethical and sustainable development of natural resources and its potential for enhancing world peace'. It took the form of an international forum, three days of serious dialogue, debate and enquiry. The event, which took place in Brisbane City Hall, was co-chaired by Mikhail Gorbachev, former President of the Soviet Union and Chair of Green Cross International, and Peter Beattie, Premier of Queensland. The aim of the forum was, as Gorbachev said in welcoming fellow delegates, 'to build a strong public consensus in support of peaceful, just and sustainable solutions to the crises which threaten our future'. Among the eminent speakers were UN special advisor, Nicholas You; from the UK, Aubrey Meyer, co-founder and Director of the Global Commons Institute, and regarded by Britain's *New Statesman* as 'one of the ten people likely to change the world'; two Nobel Peace laureates, Iranian writer and human rights activist, Dr Shirin Ebadi, and the leader of Argentina's human rights movement, Adolfo Pérez Esquivel; and Australian activists, Noel Pearson, the Reverend Tim Costello and 'Australian of the Year', Professor Ian Frazer. We were committed to resolutions, outcomes and solutions, but we had no special agenda, no expectation of what those resolutions or solutions might be. It was hugely gratifying, on the last day of the festival, to hear the Queensland Government and Brisbane City Council announce an action plan, consisting of a wide range of measures in furtherance of the forum's goals—from encouragement of the state government 'to become a regional leader in the fight against climate change, biodiversity loss, poverty and human rights violations' to urging individual citizens to 'become engaged in political processes in order to elevate sustainable development and ecological justice onto political agendas'.

The discussions that took place in *Earth Dialogues Brisbane* resonated throughout the entire festival program. Only very recently, I was very gratified to hear a woman who had been at the festival say how vividly she remembered it: 'It was amazing', she said. 'The *Earth Dialogues* discussions brought everyone together, locals and visitors, and, you might not have thought it, but it seemed entirely proper that global-warming talks should have been held at an arts festival, and an arts festival held in Brisbane.'

When visiting the festivals held on regular bases in our other state capitals, I am struck by the significant differences in their program choices and priorities. These reflect not only the tastes of the individual artistic directors, but also the differing cultures of the various regions. It is my belief that those differences should be identified and celebrated. We are all fascinated to see and hear new work, when it is brought out to these festivals from France, the UK, the USA, Asia or wherever—and a large part of that fascination is precisely that the work is *not* local, *not* familiar, but comes from a different culture. Exposing ourselves to the product of other, foreign cultures is one way of helping us define our own. We need to identify and celebrate those cultural differences more than we do at present.

4
Finding stories from our backyards

But if we are to connect in a real and meaningful way with audiences at this level, and create new work that mirrors our lives—and go on to communicate beyond its local origins—we must start at the beginning, in our own backyards. We must become attuned to the issues of concern, both the joys and the sorrows, of the people whom we wish to be included in our theatre-making process, in a word, find out what makes them tick. Then it is our responsibility to create work which is not in the first instance about national or universal issues, but which resonates immediately with the ordinary citizen, which deals with the impact of public issues on the life of the individual. This is what Aboriginal Australians have always done, told stories about their country, their people, and their everyday activities, which are then passed on by the 'story keepers' of their place.

If we can connect with our audiences locally and resonate globally we shall truly be doing something of profound importance. Many of us have given the best years of our lives to the Australian performing arts and, for most of us, much of that time has been devoted to the development of new Australian work. The majority of that work has originated in capital cities and been a reflection of metropolitan cultures. We also need to encourage the development of Australian work at a grassroots suburban and regional level. Can we not encourage the many successful amateur theatrical and music societies to create work about their towns, about their suburbs, perhaps about their own regions?

At the moment these societies seem to exist on a diet of American musicals, Gilbert and Sullivan operettas and Andrew Lloyd Webber, works that have little to do with who we are, either as Australians or as artists. It's a pity the Ministries for the Arts are unable to support those community groups in a serious manner and create opportunities for writers, directors, actors and musicians to get their hands dirty in the suburbs and the bush. Many people would be surprised to learn that one of Baz Luhrmann's first jobs on graduating from NIDA twenty years ago was directing a musical for the city of Rockhampton in central Queensland. It was called *Crocodile Creek* and people still talk about it today. It was about that place and about the people who live there; and it was tremendously successful. But one production is not enough, and there were no resources for further commissions of writers or musicians. So, inevitably, having flickered briefly, the flame died. Unfortunately, the amounts of money available under the Festivals Australia program are inadequate to sustain the development of a large-scale production. And, sadly, the Australia Council's current music committee seems unable to appreciate what is required to mount a substantial music-theatre production. Accordingly, the regional development of new music theatre is not easy.

Touring productions by major organisations should complement the activity which is already a fundamental part of the cultural life of each region or town; it should not be the only cultural activity funded to occur in that place. In my experience a production which grows from a community generates far more interest and support than a production that flies into a town for a night and, rather than making any meaningful cultural connection with that community, merely demonstrates that 'there is a world elsewhere'.

Let me use Mt Isa and the QMF again as an example. In July 2003, Oz-Opera toured to Mt Isa with Verdi's *Rigoletto*. I've no doubt that it was a fine production with a perfectly good cast—but only eighteen people attended. One month later, 18,000 people attended *Bob Cat Dancing*—and the population of Mt Isa was only 22,000 at the time! *Bob Cat Dancing* was a large-scale outdoor music-theatre piece created by QMF in association with Mt Isa City Council. Staged in the dry bed of the Leichhardt River, against a backdrop of the mine's smokestacks, the show was a tribute to the town's lifeblood industry.

Playwright Philip Dean, a man familiar with outback Queensland, fashioned a tale about a drifter who arrives in Mt Isa with special powers. 'If you can fix the bob cat', a local mechanic says to him, 'I'll give you a job'. The drifter accidentally starts the machine and quickly wins the town's acclaim as a Mr Fixit. In fact, it turns out he can talk to the machines and get them to do almost anything. And so the bob cats dance, they spin, twirl and pirouette ... Two of them, 25-tonne excavators, perform a 'love duet'; the bob cats are their progeny. John Rodgers wrote a terrific score, a mixture of country, rock, pop and gospel music, and it was played by a live band,

Bob Cat Dancing was a project of the Queensland Music Festival which we developed over eight months. It involved 155 local people—fifty of them as performers—from the Mt Isa School of Dance, Just Rock and Roll Dancers, the Harley-Davidson Riders Club, Restored Car Club, SES in Mt Isa, the Mt Isa St John's Ambulance and children from three primary schools. Such was the extraordinary success of the dancing bob cats that they had to be invited back for an encore, and for the 2005 QMF created *Bob Cat Magic*. Performed in the same dry river bed in Mt Isa, the creative team of Sven Swenson (book), John Rodgers (music), Sean Mee (director) and Ian Lawson (designer) devised a 75-minute music-theatre piece based on the Mt Isa Mardi Gras. This time the bob cats were joined by vintage cars and buses, motorcycles, BMX bikes and backhoes, and the community groups involved two years earlier were this time joined by the Mt Isa Line Dancers Association, St Joseph's Catholic School and the Mt Isa Little Theatre. Hundreds of local performers filled the many cameo roles and the massive audience took them and their magnificent dancing bob cats to their hearts. *Bob Cat Dancing* and its sister piece, *Bob Cat Magic*, are special pieces and those performances were very special times in Mt Isa for everyone.

So I am frankly alarmed to have read recently that the Perth International Arts Festival, which prides itself on being Australia's oldest and largest annual arts festival, has announced that it has cut two of the three regional centres it has visited in the past because of lack of audiences. Sad though this decision may be, it confirms everything that I've been advocating. If the work you create is not intrinsically connected to the culture of that place, it will not resonate. It is then futile to spend large amounts of money marketing a product that simply has very little support and interest from that community. If people do not feel a connection they will not attend. But if it makes that connection, if it illuminates for its audience their sense of place, then ultimately, that work can be amplified to include a greater landscape. *Bob Cat Magic* and *Bob Cat Dancing* are now so totally associated with Mt Isa that they have achieved that indefinable quality which transports a production beyond its form and place into another dimension.

That is the cultural association and effect that is necessary to build a forest of art pieces which can truly occupy the aspirations of the people who choose to live where they do. It's a celebration of the culture and the people of that place.

5
Building a cultural pyramid

I am convinced that the response to these activities reflects a profound desire and willingness to embrace new work which is grown out of the culture of place and that we have a unique opportunity to create something of lasting value.

In saying this I am not attempting to demean the classical or international work which is regularly performed by our flagship companies. Nor am I suggesting that it should be reduced in favour of more Australian work. Their achievements should be acknowledged and applauded. What I'm arguing for is a pyramid model to provide a foundation for the artistic process in which each level of artistic endeavour and appreciation can find a place. Without that foundation we are in danger of losing the steady progress of artistic output and being overruled by top-down bureaucratic manipulation.

The theatre comes from people, it is about people and people must be connected to it in their everyday lives and their everyday experiences in their backyard. We simply must encourage people to tell 'their' stories in 'their' theatres, so that we have a cultural community which supports our professional theatre practitioners, *that takes ownership of the work*.

In Mt Isa, a board member of QMF was keen to be taken on a tour of the great Mt Isa Mine. He arrived late and, although the mine guide had no idea who he was, he said, 'OK, I'll take you, but first, are you coming to our show tonight?' 'Our show'—the most joyous words I could have heard. Eighteen thousand people took ownership of *Bob Cat Magic*. They had never heard of the composer, the writer, the director or anyone (apart from the locals) in the cast, but it was still their own. Two new large-scale Australian works were commissioned and performed in 2003 and 2005 playing to 36,000 people—here there is clearly something happening,

Similarly, in Charters Towers in 2005 I commissioned Janis Balodis to write the text and Shenton Gregory to compose the music for *Charters Towers—The Musical*, a celebration of the history and culture of the Dalrymple Shire and the north Queensland mining town —'Charlie's Trousers', as it is known colloquially. Twelve months before the event I set out to talk about the culture of place, give the piece a name and negotiate a deal with both the Dalrymple Shire Council and the Charters Towers City Council. The event took place in the town's main street—closed off on each of the three performance evenings—on a three-tier stage erected in front of the recently renovated Royal Private Hotel, one of the town's historic pubs. We worked with 200 local performers for four months and brought in a couple of stars, Annie Lee and Ian Stenlake. Kathryn Sproul built an enormous set and designed fabulous costumes. Scott Maidment directed this huge show and the result was extraordinary. The first night was rained out, but it didn't stop about fifteen hundred people turning up to see what would happen! There were two more performances and 10,000 more people poured into Charters Towers to see 'their' musical.

Later, the CEO of Charters Towers City Council wrote to us:

> On behalf of Council I would welcome the opportunity to hold a similar event at any time and I think it would be a wonderful venture to hold similar events throughout all Queensland towns and cities, and indeed nationally. Although I realise this would be a costly and time-consuming venture, I think the cultural, social and economic rewards would far exceed these limitations, particularly if carried out with the skill and expertise that was displayed in our particular instance.

And from the Community Development Officer for the Dalrymple Shire Council: '*Charters Towers—The Musical* has left a legacy that we believe is still dancing and singing its way around the streets and hearts of all that were involved.'

As we all know, this is not a common reaction. There is a wave of ownership for original, inventive Australian work which is firmly grounded in the culture of place which genuinely wants to be heard and we simply must support this new energy. All the councils who were part of the Queensland Music Festival contributed substantial amounts of cash and in-kind support to these projects. They were part of the commissioning, workshopping and auditioning process—and, of course, the production itself. At the QMF in 2005 we played in twenty-three centres, and in seventeen of these new work was created that reflected the particular community and its culture. It is interesting to reflect on how our cultural landscape might be affected if we were able to expand still further, and create, say, thirty new pieces in thirty different communities. Of one thing I am sure: if the new Artistic Director of the Queensland Music Festival in 2007 does not commission a new work for Charters Towers, questions will be asked in the Queensland Parliament!

■

The more new work we produce, the less likely we are to place high expectations on it. We seem to be obsessed with creating 'masterpieces', and look to every new work to justify its existence by being an instant success. The expectation that every new work will be a 'product', and not simply part of an ongoing creative 'process', can put intolerable pressure on artists. The fault, however, lies not with the arts community but with their funding bodies and with an economy that would rather finance in a one-off, ad hoc manner than provide continuing support to ongoing research and developmental work. (Our scientists have similar problems—though on a much larger scale—and so are forced to leave and work in greener pastures overseas.) But there's no denying that the arts suffer badly in the prevailing outcome-based culture.

In 2002 I set up the first Creative Laboratory in Australia at NORPA. This has produced a number of important productions that have received national acclaim, most recently *The Drover's Wives* at the 2006 Perth International Arts Festival. It allowed artists to work in a theatre, with technicians; they were provided with accommodation and they were allowed the time and facilities they needed to develop a new work. This was funded by the NSW Ministry for the Arts. However, in 2005 the funding for the Laboratory was discontinued—a serious error of judgment on the part of the Ministry, I believe. Research needs to be continuous and ongoing, not erratic and ad hoc, project by project, as it is at present.

What I've been trying to develop in the preceding pages is the idea of a cultural pyramid, on top of whose broad-based foundation our professional performing arts industry might sit, and upon whose work our professional companies might feed. The work I'm talking about, of course, is the kind of project developed and enjoyed in regional Queensland, at Charters Towers, Winton, Mt Isa, in Lismore with NORPA and at the Brisbane Festival. After involvement in a local venture of this sort, Australian artists would grow up with a heightened sense of place, a clearer understanding of their particular culture and a 'connection' to stories about themselves as individuals and about their town, their suburb, their community. If the work presented by our professional companies were created by artists imbued with spirit of this kind and accustomed to community project work, then it might become more adventurous, brave and daring. It is to be hoped that this in turn might encourage new audiences to come to the theatre, audiences for whom theatre would be less of a foreign country, more of an extension of their own backyard.

The work undertaken at the summit of our pyramid by the professional companies might challenge the conventional or traditional idea of theatre, but it could provide audiences with experiences and sensations that were life-changing. This is the area which is about the brave new world of communications art, where technology links individual and local theatre processes to a global community which could enable scenes from New York, Europe, Asia and the Southern Hemisphere to be part of a genuine world or international production. Technology could be used to serve a truly world-wide communications theatre event which would be grounded in the intimate experiences of individual cultures.

6
So what is community?

All this, however, depends on restoring or rediscovering our sense of community in the arts. It is essential that we try to listen to the new voices, the small innovations, the new ideas that at present are unable to make themselves heard amid the hubbub of cultural confusion.

Within that context of community I would like to quote from the late Nick Enright, who in his 2002 Rex Cramphorn Lecture said:

> It is that notion of community which is part of my theme today. It is the sense of calm and communal creativity, the serious yet entirely playful focus on a common goal whose ultimate aim is communication with the wider community, the audience. I believe we have largely lost that sense of community and with it the sense of enterprise, initiative and collaboration.

Some of what I'm trying to say, others have said before me. But I do believe that we are at a very important time in our short theatre-making history. If we continue to try to replicate in our theatres what can be seen on television, we will die. We need to identify our sense of place, and make work about that place and about the people who inhabit it in a brave, bold, creative and stimulating manner. I'm speaking about communicating the essential truth that is the core of any worthwhile theatrical experience. And in doing this we need to have the courage to be clear and simple in our storytelling. I don't mean that we should 'dumb down' what we do—far from it.

Some time ago, in an interview for the arts newspaper, *RealTime*, I said how heartened I had been by the fact that we had programmed work that attracted larger audiences in Lismore than in Sydney—work by Elision, for example, the contemporary music ensemble, who don't produce the 'easiest' work. Not only that, I said, but the larger arts organisations presume that, if you live in the bush, your IQ must be a lot lower than if you live in the metropolitan area. That's nonsense, of course, but it is the case that country people have much less access than city people to cultural activity. Festivals like the QMF offer opportunities to expose them to all sorts of work—shows such as *Bob Cat Dancing*, but also more complex and demanding work. The important thing is that the local community feel some connection to it, and ideally that the process of creating the work actively engages them.

I am advocating a whole host of individual communities actively participating in the making of art and in supporting a community of artists; whether as individuals, as members of the grassroots community with our professional theatre companies, or in the brave new world of advanced technology This means playing not just to, or for, our fellow artists. The wider community must also be engaged.

The co-op performances I've seen in Sydney recently are full of vitality and vigour; they are pushing the boundaries, seeking fresh modes of expression. It's vibrant, exciting work, and it reminds me very much of the rough-and-tumble performances that were such an essential part of the theatre-making process in Sydney and Melbourne during the 1970s. Sometimes, though we have acquired some marvellous theatre buildings since those heady days, I think we may have lost some of that essential Australian larrikin style so essential to our theatrical expression. We have become a bit too comfortable, even a bit blasé, in our attitudes to fully engage with our cultural personality and that in turn has an effect on the work we make and how we play it. I believe that our personality is determined primarily by place, and its importance in the make-up of who we are cannot be overstated.

Perversely, David Williamson's work is often criticised for its popularity and its appeal to audiences, but no one can deny that it connects with an enormously wide demographic and carries his audiences from the broad grassroots base to the upper layers of the pyramid. In that sense, in the audiences' mind there is no separation between amateur and professional productions.

To develop further what I'm advocating, a re-assessment of our perceived view of the relationship between amateur and professional organisations is needed. We need to look at the rough origins of our theatre and where we have taken it in the last thirty years. Then we might begin to see with new insight and different criteria of judgment the store of energy contained in life outside our capitals. We might begin to acquire a regional state of mind. We need an open debate about the relative importance of quality in performance and connection to community.

■

Issues of national importance are not being debated on our main stages today and I find this disappointing. It's worrying that the same faces appear at most arts events and that the percentage of our population that goes to the theatre is pathetic. In Brisbane I've been shocked to discover how few suburban residents have been to the Queensland Performing Arts Centre; I'm sure the statistic would be similar in other capitals. Those venues are simply not on the radar for most of our population. 'Too expensive', 'I don't go into the city very often' or 'I have no interest in it' are some of the most common responses.

The fact is that we have built for ourselves a top-down bureaucratic system of arts and cultural methodology and, unless we reverse it, we will continue to be frustrated by the state of the profession to which so many of us have given the best years of our lives. So many of the wonderful Australian works we have had the privilege to perform will be lost. What we have to say as artists and human beings about our society is already being drowned by American films, pop music and internet performances. The broad-based pyramid will sink into a suburban desert.

I don't want this to happen in Australia. We have far more interesting stories to tell. We have a mighty resource of talented individuals who genuinely want to make a difference to our cultural life and we need to examine why our community is less interested now than it has ever been in the work being created. Is it that we have become so seduced by the glitz of globalisation that we no longer notice how our own culture, like our own landscape, is being eroded?

Are we not aware how many imported productions are franchises in the same category as McDonald's? Exactly the same ingredients and packaging in every city in the world—is that really what we want? A new creation, on the other hand, is unique. It belongs at a particular address. It's a window into a special moment in time and a special experience. That is not the case with a 'one show fits all' philosophy.

The disappearance of languages, like that of unique animal and plant species, is a tragedy which seems to pass without notice or regret. Our accent is becoming more and more 'mid-Atlantic'. It was once such a beautiful, broad, sardonic drawl (that is still seductive to many Americans), but television, pop music, films and 'internet/text speak' are rapidly eroding one of the pillars of our culture.

If we lose our accent and our way of using language we really will become another city somewhere off the west coast of the USA. So every piece that genuinely has the potential to reveal afresh to the world the culture, the people and the substance of our place can play a part in staving off that day. It's worth considering that if we fail to question, if we continue to do things the way we have always done, we will always get what we've always had.

7
Management structures: do they need to change?

Over the past thirty years, while business organisations have been experimenting with new models of management, the structure of arts organisations has remained fundamentally the same—artistic director, general manager, reporting to a board and managing down. The business world has been far more creative in management structure than we in the artistic community. It is common for a business to restructure every few years as the organisation responds to the marketplace and to its business and public environment. It is rare for arts organisations to do this.

The current ideas regarding arts management are old-fashioned, cumbersome, authoritarian and not as effective as they could, or should, be. Some companies are in the preposterous situation of having a CEO or a general manager, but no artistic director. It's the equivalent of having a football team without a coach! How does this affect the making of Australian art? Ultimately, the fundamental driver of every arts organisation is the art we make and the program we produce. If an arts organisation loses sight of that purpose and comes to believe that maintaining its own bureaucracy is its reason for being, then there is little point in its existing.

By relying on an outdated form of management we stifle the creative growth of the company. It inhibits the making of progressive work because it does not provide the structure for a springboard to creativity. We need to address the mechanism which governs the creative process and devise contemporary management structures which are more democratic and inclusive, reflecting the kind of cultural pyramid I'm proposing, and which will give the art the freedom it needs to grow. In other words, a creative management structure will provide first the security and then the impetus for imaginative artistic creativity. If IT companies can do it, why not the arts?

A creative management structure allows more people to grow within the organisation and more aspirations to be addressed. People are our finest resource and it's imperative that the people who make the organisation are able to develop and achieve their goals. We would then celebrate a management culture that was constantly growing and achieving, rather than aging and rusting.

Some arts organisations, of course, function with a very small core-management team and it would be difficult for them to implement my suggestion. But for larger arts organisations and festivals I would advocate a modular structure, i.e. a range of autonomous departments, each managed by its own director, enjoying the freedom to work creatively, but also operating as a team in delivering the season or the festival. Within a structure such as this the management becomes part of the creative process, so that everyone is liberated from the bureaucratic structures which inhibit the creation of exciting new work. This also breaks down the silos of division which stifle creativity in many larger arts organisations.

In recent times there has been an increasing tendency towards over-regulation. Every arts company must be fiscally responsible, and scrupulously so, but there is a world of difference between finding reasons why a project can't be done and finding reasons to make the project possible. Unfortunately, risk management strategies and contractual restrictions have taken control in some instances and are choking the life out of the process of making art.

By contrast, the modular structure I'm advocating ensures that the gatekeeper's responsibilities are shared by the directors of the various departments within the organisation. This means that the bottleneck that frequently occurs at the top can be expanded to accommodate the maximum traffic. All the controls and insurances remain in place, but the responsibility of control is evenly distributed across the senior management of the organisation. It is vital for us to develop such alternative and more creative management structures and strategies. This applies particularly to major festivals.

8
Who are we, the audience?

What is the role of the audience in our pyramid of artistic expression? Are we making art which is self-indulgent? Is the concept of excellence related directly to the complexity or incomprehensibility of the work?

The infrastructure imposed today by the artistic process at the highest level too often results in theatre companies, dance companies, opera companies and orchestras contracting in size and scope. That translates into unimaginative work of poor quality which further alienates audiences and, just as importantly, sponsors and supporters. We must have an audience to play to or the art forms we cherish will wither and die.

At this time of national questioning, the notion of what is Australian is pertinent. If we are questioning what that fundamental means, then we will surely question what community means to all of us. Community is a connection, sometimes an identifiable catalyst, a common understanding, that underlines our fundamental sense of belonging. As artists, our responses to the different cultural messages within a community determine the creative and artistic impulses we are able to communicate. These impulses translate individually and collectively. They represent a collective group as well as particular individuals. The eventual performance is the cultural expression of not only particular artists, but ideally the culture of that particular place as it is reflected through that community.

As an Australian community we have evolved and been transformed quite dramatically over the past thirty years. The changes which have taken place in our appreciation of good food and wine for example have been dramatic. Our tastes in literature, art, theatre and music have also changed. But are our tastes more sophisticated and intelligent now than they were thirty years ago? I would suggest that our appreciation for the making of new Australian work in contemporary dance and contemporary classical music is not as enthusiastic as it was during the 1970s. Are we less adventurous or are we finding adventure in different, more 'modern', more technological ways? On the contrary, I believe that greater breadth of choice has made us more conservative.

How can this be? It has become clear, to those who observe these things, that much of the work created in these forms in recent times rarely connects to a community. In consequence, the audience that once existed has become disillusioned and has turned away. Even when there is work of importance created, it struggles to find an audience because the corporate memory of that audience remains sceptical and disillusioned. This applies particularly to contemporary dance, but also in part to contemporary classical music.

Perhaps structure should receive fresh consideration in provisions for subsidy. Rather than providing 'funding' and giving 'grants', perhaps the relevant Ministries for the Arts and the Australia Council could investigate 'investing' in projects and individual artists, with a view to a negotiated return on the investment. The return need not necessarily be financial, but rather the endorsement of the community that has engaged in the enterprise and supports the investment.

Whatever mechanism is employed, it is imperative that we commit to engaging with our various communities and allowing our potential audience to be passionate and proud of the art we are making.

9
How do we pay for it?

This, of course, is the question which will always be asked. But the better one is, 'How do we value culture?' Do we put a price on the legacy of Sir Donald Bradman, on Anzac Day, the commemoration of Gallipoli? Do we put a price on the cultural life of outback towns like Mt Isa, Charters Towers, Barcaldine or somewhere like Normanton? As taxpayers, do those of us who choose to live in those towns have fewer cultural rights than our cousins in Sydney and Melbourne? It may be that our preferred cultural fascination is not classical theatre or grand opera, but there is nothing wrong with that. What matters is that we be encouraged to act in our own way, sing to our own tunes. The fact that I have earned my living by singing opera around the world for the past thirty years does not prevent me from defending the rights of those who find opera elitist and alien. A marimba band, a musical about Charters Towers, or a show with dancing bob cats, might have infinitely more to say and resonate far more movingly than *Rigoletto*, with certain audiences. This is exactly as it should be, and these audience preferences deserve to be supported with public funding every bit as much as Opera Australia.

But how and to what extent are we to fund the sort of cultural activities I've been concerned with here? Should Mt Isa's bob-cat culture receive the same generous level of support as ballet, opera, theatre and symphonic music? If not, then why not? Are we content to be mortgaged to the sustenance of imported European art forms, at the expense of the development of an authentic local culture? These questions need urgent answers.

Perhaps a discrete Australia Council board is needed to handle professional arts activity that is particular to places situated more than 200 kilometres from a capital city. I am constantly surprised by the extent to which 'place' or 'location' is ignored as a factor in the formulation of public arts policy. At the Cultural Ministers' Conference held in New Zealand in September 2006, money for regional touring was increased, despite the evidence that it might have been better spent on new work that originated in the regions, was about those regions and developed wholly or in part by locals there. Not that the responsibility need always be sheeted home to the Australia Council. Perhaps local government, local councils, need greater encouragement to co-operate with one another in actively promoting local arts and culture. The Queensland Music Festivals provide ample evidence of what can be achieved by a number of local councils all coming to the party.

I'm not, I hasten to add, suggesting that we rob Peter to pay Paul. I'm advocating a re-examination of the principles upon which decisions are made regarding fund-distribution to the cultures of the many different places that constitute Australia and the people who are the products of those cultures. I'm suggesting that for Australia in 2007 arts funding at all levels is inadequate and its allocation ill-directed; not only is it insufficient for the development and continued sustainment of original, culturally based arts activity, but there is too great a propensity to fund metropolitan projects.

Outside the government sector, other areas of support are available. And here there is opportunity for much more personal involvement. But how are we to boost the aid that comes from the philanthropic sector, which is so limited here in Australia, compared to that of the USA? Is it because too few have experience of the potential offered by the non-metropolitan sector? Or too little understanding of the process which produces original artistic work in general? The private sector is a serious source of income, but remains a very small pool and the same generous individuals are looked to by everyone for assistance.

It is embarrassing to recall the QMF's wonderful Cooktown Celebration in 2005, with artists from the Solomon Islands, the Huli Wigmen from Papua New Guinea, local artists and schoolchildren and community members. It was a very special experience for everyone involved and had a profound effect on the Cooktown community. While we raised significant amounts of money from a number of local sources, our primary support came from America—in the form of a very generous US$100,000 grant from the Christensen Fund in California. Why did an American philanthropic foundation support a cultural event on the other side of the world, enabling thirty distinguished Melanesian musicians to take part? Because it is their purpose 'to focus their grant-making on the interface between natural environment and human culture'. They acknowledge the value of fostering the relationship between people and place, and believe in the contribution the arts can make in bringing people together.

Now, since the Federal Government began to offer philanthropists generous incentives in the form of charity tax concessions, there has been a marked upward trend in Australian philanthropy: in the six years from 1995 to 2001 alone, the total value of individual tax-deductible donations rose from $500 million to more than $800 million. But we in the arts community must be more proactive. Whoever said this was right: 'Money is not given, it has to be raised; it is not offered, it has to be asked for.' Of course, we must help would-be philanthropists to understand the aims and achievements of diverse cultural processes and celebration, and the great benefits of community-building initiatives such as the Cooktown Celebration. But we can go further: we can urge them to deeds of practical generosity by acquiring tax-deductible status, by registering as a charity receiving tax-exemption or by forming a partnership with a registered arts organisation that already has such an exemption.

10
A cultural revolution

Australia's regionality, the view of its regional strength and diversity within a global context, is part of the scenario I've outlined in the preceding pages. The cultural climate in Australia today is very different from that of thirty years ago. At that time the very idea that one might make a career as an opera singer was utterly preposterous. Today, such a choice would no longer provoke ridicule. We have an opera house that is world famous, and every state has its own symphony orchestra, state theatre company, ballet and opera company. But do these organisations really reflect the cultural preferences of most Australians in 2007? Or are we clinging to the last vestiges of the European art forms to which some of our parents and grandparents were so attached? With the dramatically changing demographic that characterises contemporary Australia, and with the shift in population centres, has come a shift in cultural and artistic preferences.

Some of these changes relate to the movement of the demographic centre of Sydney to Parramatta and the western suburbs of Sydney, and of the fifteen hundred people who migrate from elsewhere in Australia to Brisbane and south-east Queensland every week. These are dramatic population shifts. By 2010, we are told, Brisbane will have become a larger city than Melbourne. What might the impact of that be on the cultural balance of Australia?

If Queensland's cultural identity continues to develop as it has done, very differently from that of Victoria, then the balance of current practice will be challenged. It will begin a revolution in the way the community demands that cultural activity should be supported. We may well find that an opera company is not as essential to every Australian city as was previously thought.

In twenty-first-century Australia, will a city's artistic credibility still be dependent on whether it has a symphony orchestra and an opera company? Or will this change in demographic distribution mean that, say, Chinese opera is more culturally relevant? Perhaps there is already a different cultural heritage calling for attention, and which is part of a broader cultural and artistic landscape. We need to be awake to these possibilities in looking to the future.

The cultural pyramid I've described will provide the foundation for a new model of cultural and artistic democracy, one that is much more sympathetic to

Australian thinking than the hierarchy we have at present—and one that will insist that our cultural identity be defined by the community. Some of the responses will be dictated by demographic shifts and very different cultural preferences. Some will be governed by artistic necessity.

However, for the cultural life of Australia to genuinely connect to the broadest possible community, and for those communities who at present feel disenfranchised to know that they are culturally and artistically represented, we all need to feel ownership of a national cultural laboratory. A state where, artistically, anything is possible, where art is valued, where experimentation is respected, where the cultures of numerous regions and areas are encouraged to raise their voices and where uniqueness is prized, not ridiculed.

The world seen from Cooktown is very different from that seen from Brisbane and it's important for us all to recognise—and to value—that difference, if our regional state of mind is to become a state of cultural and artistic maturity. It should be sophisticated in form and methodology and responsive to the simplest needs of its community, but essentially it should be culturally democratic and artistically resplendent.

Readers' Forum

Response to Stuart Cunningham's Platform Papers No. 9, *What Price a Creative Economy?*

Robert Beveridge teaches media policy at Napier University in Edinburgh. He is also Director of Voice of the Listener and Viewer, a media advocacy group for quality, diversity and a secure future for public service broadcasting.

Stuart Cunningham's essay—indeed, each of the quarterly *Platform Papers*—deserves a global readership, not least because it is important that we take the debate from seeing and deploying arguments for public and private money for the arts, culture and creativity as being subsidies and more as investing in economic success and quality of life issues.

However, it is important not to assume that the new digital technologies are such that the arguments and policies that have served for the analogue world can be jettisoned in their entirety. Of course, Cunningham does not call for this, and nothing is more poignant than his reminder that, while we need to understand the 'interaction between the potent legacy of broadcasting and the convergent broadband media, [...] content creation [needs to] remain close to the mainstream of popular cultural consumption' (p. 41).

Yet the market—or, if you like, audience taste—is formed in part by what is made available and by the judgments of the creative artists and community in their attempts to communicate their visions and ideas to themselves and to their audiences/readerships. And here the real enemy of creativity is marketing. Too powerful an impetus towards giving the audience what they will want leads to repeating forms and formulas. Alternatively, trying to be so sensational and controversial means that the real aim becomes that of publicity and competing for attention in an overcrowded marketplace.

Furthermore, the arrival of digitalisation will certainly extend the number of channels but will it really extend choice and diversity? In my judgment, not if it is accompanied by further deregulation and an increasing tendency to conceptualise the viewer/listener/online creator or contributor as a consumer, rather than as a citizen who should have a range of entitlements.

Here Cunningham is absolutely right to call for linkages which establish 'tripartite interfaces between cultural institutions, universities and content industries' (p. 40). This is particularly needed, not least because small-scale independent enterprises frequently lack the capacity and capital to enable them to undertake sufficient investment in education and training for their staff.

So creativity depends on having organisational cultures which can remember, celebrate and use the best of the past while not being bound by it, and find new but quality ways of determining the new—not just new for its own sake, but new with meaning and resonance.

And this also needs perhaps to be a mixture of the global and the local, so that, as Cunningham so clearly indicates, each city or economy can share and jointly develop ideas and frameworks. I know that many in Scotland and elsewhere would love to join in such ventures.

Finally, it might be worth recalling the maxim of a former Director-General of the BBC, who called for the Corporation to 'make the popular good and the good popular'. Despite Cunningham's tempting dismissal of essential arguments—a position which is articulated in the 1940s Powell and

Pressburger film, *The Life and Death of Colonel Blimp*, and, yes, the music of Beethoven and Mozart did not prevent Nazism—nonetheless, the story of progress, while very uneven, does lead to an acknowledgement of the positive power of the BBC's (and the ABC's) mission to inform, educate and entertain and, nowadays, to connect—in every sense of the word.

So, we in Scotland look forward to further, and extended, connection with Australian ideas and platforms.

Responses to Jonathan Biggins' Platform Papers No. 10, *Satire—or Sedition? The Threat to National Insecurity*

Professor George Williams and Edwina MacDonald are based at the Gilbert + Tobin Centre of Public Law, University of New South Wales.

We enjoyed reading Jonathan Biggins' discussion of the role of satire in political commentary and the threat posed to satire by the new sedition laws.

On 13 November last, at a forum hosted by the Human Rights and Equal Opportunity Commission, Attorney-General Philip Ruddock indicated that the sedition offences were not intended to capture artists and media commentators. He pointed to the requirement that a person must intend to urge another person to use force and violence, and the existence of good faith defences as factors that limit the application of the offences. However, as Biggins and the Australian Law Reform Commission point out, there is no requirement that a person intend that the violence actually occur. Further, the good faith defences are limited to situations where a person is trying to engage in reform or point out errors in laws, policies or actions. It is possible that some satire—for example, a parody of Osama Bin Laden, where a person intentionally urges particular action but does not intend that anyone follow that action—would risk contravening a sedition offence.

While it is unlikely that an artist or satirist will be prosecuted for sedition, ultimately it comes down to the discretion of the prosecutors and the Attorney-General as to whether to lay charges. This is not satisfactory. It is unacceptable to rely on the selective application of a law by politicians and others to ensure that blameless people do not become criminals. As well as being bad law, the risk of breaking the law—even if it won't lead to prosecution—can result in self-censorship, an issue Biggins discusses in detail in his essay.

Hindsight was not necessary to identify that there are problems with the sedition law. When the law was passed by Parliament in late 2005, people from all sides of politics believed it to be flawed. In spite of this, the law was still passed but the government agreed to have the law reviewed by the Australian Law Reform Commission. The Commission released its final report on 13 September 2006 with recommendations along the lines of those in the discussion paper referred to by Biggins. Two months later, as we write, the government is yet to respond. However, Ruddock has indicated that he does not agree with the recommendation that an intention that the urged force or violence will occur should be a part of the offences.

Australia needs anti-terror laws, but they must be the right ones to ensure our security and to protect our fundamental freedoms. The object of new terror laws cannot be national security at all costs. They can only be justified to the extent that they protect our democratic freedoms and way of life, something that is made more difficult by the lack of a national charter of rights.

Like the sedition law, many of our anti-terror laws have been enacted and amended with great speed with little time for public or parliamentary debate. Reviews of the law can provide a way for us to examine our anti-terror laws and ensure we have the best laws possible. But the government must be prepared to consider and implement the recommendations from such reviews. If they refuse to do so, we may be left with laws that unnecessarily erode our freedoms without protecting us from the threat of terrorism.

Robyn Nevin is Artistic Director of Sydney Theatre Company.

In 1999, in the euphoric moments after my appointment to the Sydney Theatre Company, I called Ruth Cracknell. I knew I wanted to start a political revue, had lit upon Jonathan Biggins as the possible front man and wanted to offer him the chance to develop it. But first I checked with Australia's undisputed queen of comedy. 'He's perfect', Ruth offered. Perfect seemed good enough. Jonathan was appointed as Artistic Director, STC *Wharf Revue*. And so it came into being.

My early references were the *Phillip Street Revue*, TV's *The Mavis Bramston Show* and *That Was the Week That Was*, and more recently, back in a live space, Kinselas' revue shows. I was around when Leon Fink's entrepreneurial genius excited into life that former funeral parlour in Taylor Square, making it a buzzy, relevant restaurant bar and cabaret room. For five years Sydney flocked to the room upstairs where Patrick Cook cartooned live; Max Gillies outed Bob Hawke, Russ Hinze and the Queen; Los Trios Ringbarkus barked; Garry McDonald's awful creation, Phil Stein, was born; the Globos spawned Mark Trevorrow's comic persona Bob Downe. Barry Humphries sent a letter of support. David Williamson took his cast there for supper after his latest premiere, Max Lambert and Linda Nagle played and sang. Brett Whiteley ate there. It felt immediate, a place to be, a kind of artistic nerve centre. Very Sydney.

That was the inspiration for my *Wharf Revue*. But I wanted a consistent team, to offer, through sharp writing and performance, an immediate sense of our political climate now. I believed 'the boys', Jonathan with Drew Forsythe and Phil Scott, had the talent to make it work. And they always added a fabulous woman to the mix, Genevieve Lemon, Valerie Bader, Linda Nagle…

The opening *Revue* set a tone of glorious silliness, *The End of the Wharf As We Know It*, and we knew that our Wharf, the site of serious theatre in Sydney, would never be the same again. It had been invaded by a comic satiric virus. Fine by me. But fun though the early ones were, it took a few shows before they began to gain confidence in their collective abilities to offer serious political satire. Once the more risky stuff started we kept an eye on the legal implications, led by our board director and legal expert, Henric Nicholas. Our board was emphatically supportive of the team's freedom to satirise, but the *Revue* sailed close to the wind a couple of times, and inevitably incurred wrath in certain quarters.

Over seven years it has evolved into a real force, a brilliant satirical revue team, confidently shining its collective light on our political leaders and commentators, and anyone or anything they reckon needs attention. In 2005 and 2006 our audience observed the increasingly dark tone of the *Revue* content. They are glad of the deepening and darkening focus of the writing. They say with satisfaction, 'This is in response to our times'. What greater praise than that they reflect the nation's tone?

The legislation which Jonathan examines in his essay unnerved us, admittedly. Not for fear we would be prosecuted but for fear we might slip into self-censorship. As a theatre company we have a responsibility to our artists to facilitate their need to express themselves in their own voices, and to our audiences to let them hear those diverse voices. This is a fundamental responsibility for free speech which I am confident will prevail.